101 Things to Do in
Shipshewana

101 Things to Do in Shipshewana

Copyright 2010
Melissa Troyer

ISBN 978-0-615-35643-3
First edition - 2010

Published by Harmony Marketing
Middlebury, IN 46540

Manufactured in the United States of America

Don't overlook
life's small joys
while searching
for the big ones.

Nearly 500 residents call Shipshewana home, and many of the one million annual travelers who sojourn here wish that they, too, could call it home. Locals hold their blessed heritage close to their hearts, while visitors admire and even long for this simpler way of life. "Shipshe," as we call it, means many things to many different people, but it mostly symbolizes simplicity.

I've known Shipshewana all my life, from a treasured vantage point of varied perspectives. My father's family broke away from the Amish church when he was seven years old. Extended family reunions are a rich tradition for our family, attended by kin with belief systems ranging from Old-Order Amish to progressive "English," the term used locally for those who are anything other than Amish. Growing up in the area, I had the privilege of knowing its people and its places first hand. Living elsewhere for a number of years gave me the chance to view the area's charms through the lens of a visitor. Working in tourism marketing for the past ten years has provided copious opportunities to share Shipshewana's stories with others.

The stories in this book weave together the melody of a rich collection of voices. This book was created in partnership with the Shipshewana Retail Merchants Association, where I served as executive director from 2003 to 2007. With their support, I have sifted through hundreds of places, activities, events and nuggets of information. The Shipshewana area is celebrated for being home to the third-largest Amish community in the United States, for having the Midwest's largest flea market, and for its reputation for hand-crafted wares. This book celebrates these better-known attributes, and furthermore reveals the lesser-known gems that can only be uncovered by venturing onto the back roads. I offer this compilation of tales, gathered from the inside voices, as a guide to enrich your visit by learning a little bit more about the area's simple beauty, generous people and deep traditions.

Most area businesses are family-owned. In keeping with local religious traditions, you'll find that most businesses are closed Sundays, and that many shops shut down in time for the owners to join their families for dinner. Sundays and evenings are great times to enjoy the beautiful parks and scenic drives; I've included a few in the book. This list is intended to whet your appetite and help make the most of your time in Shipshewana. You can find more details at www.Shipshewana.com.

My wish for you is that your time spent in the Shipshewana area will renew and refresh your spirit, and that your treasured souvenirs include precious memories and new friendships.

1

Start at the very beginning

Menno-Hof is the best place to start your pursuit of learning the ins and outs of Shipshewana. Take a hands-on journey through the unique history of Amish and Mennonite cultures as 28 display areas and narrative exhibits, including the tornado theater, dungeon room, sailing ship, and play loft, bring the culture to life before your eyes. Plenty of local guides are on hand to personally answer questions. Menno-Hof also has a great gift shop and book store. Beautiful gardens, including the floral Quilt Garden, are on display here seasonally. Want a sneak peek? Take a virtual tour on the Menno-Hof website.

510 S Van Buren St, Shipshewana
260.768.4117
www.MennoHof.org

2

Fine furniture *and* craftsmanship

People travel from hundreds of miles to purchase handcrafted furniture made by local Amish woodworkers. Furniture making has recently become such a large industry that the Northern Indiana Woodcrafters Association, that started with just a handful of member business in 2000, now has grown to over 80 members. Some woodworkers specialize in parts like seats, legs and backs, while others create entire pieces of furniture and cabinetry. Custom kitchens and baths are a thriving local industry as well. Venture into some of the shops and you'll find one that carries your favorite style – traditional or modern. The dovetail drawers, mortise and tenon joints and hand-rubbed finishes are traditions passed down through generations of woodworkers. This heirloom-quality furniture is crafted one piece at a time, so special-orders are usually welcomed.

3

The roads less traveled

Once you understand the local road numbering system, it's pretty easy to maneuver. Except for areas with lakes, most of the roads are on a grid system. The county line runs north and south between Middlebury and Shipshewana, which is where you'll see that the roads change names. Don't worry too much about it. Even if your "Sunday Drive" happens on a weekday, folks along the way are happy to share directions, and free maps and brochures are easy to find at most businesses.

Bid boldly. Bag bargains. Attend an auction.

The first auction in town was in 1922, when six pigs, seven cows and several head of young cattle were sold at the home of George Curtis. Today, local auctions sell everything from tack to toys and livestock to living rooms. Check out local papers for weekly and specialty auctions. Perennial auctions include:

- Chupp's Annual Toy Auction, January
- Yoder's Consignment Auction, April
- Topeka Carriage Auction, April & October
- Antique and Livestock Auctions, Wednesdays
- Horse and Tack Auction, Fridays

800.254.8090
www.VisitShipshewana.org

5

Visit the toymaker's shop

It's a quiet drive to Owl Toy Craft. The shop sits on a very narrow dirt road, and as you pull into the drive, as directed by the sign, you'll wonder if you're actually at the right place. Rest assured that the shop is tucked in behind the barn, and if you are looking for traditional wooden toys, you've found the right place. Owen Wingard and his family design and handcraft all of the toys at their shop. Depending on the day, you may be able to actually watch the Wingards as they work. These are simple, unpainted, wooden toys: tractors, trains, barns, marble rollers, grain elevators, wagons, buggies and wooden fences. Their form and function appeal to all kids, young and old.

9555 W 300 S, Topeka
260.593.2651

6

Life lessons

For me, the most precious sights in the Shipshewana area are the unexpected scenes discovered while driving past a countryside Amish school. You may happen upon the whole school playing a game of baseball or kickball in the early hours while the teacher is preparing for the day, or kids might be eating their home-packed lunches in the yard. You'll know school is in session and "scholars" (the term still used today) are busy at work if you see a row of bicycles lined up next to the teacher's buggy, warm smoke coming from the chimney on cool days, and simple, well-loved playground swings waiting for recess time.

7

Everyone goes to JoJo's

Twenty years ago, Levi & JoJo (JoAnna) King started rolling dough, and now, on a busy day, JoJo's makes over 1,000 hand-rolled pretzels. This destination is well-loved by many people, with everyone having their own favorite combination of the seven different pretzel varieties and sweet and savory toppings. Little known fact: their wheat flour is locally ground. School groups often come in to hear the history of the pretzel. One tale claims that a monk twisted the dough to resemble children praying as they cross their arms on their chests. Another story points to monks using the pretzel's inter-connected loops to help children grasp the concept of the Holy Trinity.

Davis Mercantile, first floor
260.768.7759
www.ShipshewanaShops.com

8

Whoopie!

Looking like a huge cake-like Oreo, whoopie pies are a favorite local treat. A whoopie pie is like a sandwich, but made with two soft cookies, usually chocolate but sometimes pumpkin, and filled with white, fluffy cream. According to Amish legend, when children would find these goodies in their lunch bags, they would shout, "Whoopie!" You'll find whoopie pies in most local bakeries, and even at roadside stands if you're lucky. If you want to try your hand at making them, check out local Amish cookbooks, available in many shops.

9

Search for hidden treasure

Grab your GPS and tromp through 120 acres of northern hardwood forest at Maple Wood Nature Center to find a hidden geocache; when you've uncovered the treasure, drop in a trinket and take one to keep for yourself! Maple Wood is a treasure in itself, with miles of hiking trails and popular educational programs all year. The Nature Center has a full wall of windows, where critters that walk, fly and slither come out of the woods to visit. Interpretative Naturalist Scott Beam says the land is home to a wide array of animals, including those

that are rare, endangered, and common, but hard to see. Keep an eye out for deer, birds, raccoon, turkey and even red fox. Open all year, seven days a week.

4550 E 100 S, LaGrange
260.463.4022
www.LaGrangeCountyParks.org

10

Really get away from it all

The Farmstead Bed & Breakfast presents a rare opportunity to actually stay at an Amish home. You'll stay in the Dawdy Haus, the extension of the home where the grandparents traditionally live, and can freely roam the farm and even help with chores if you'd like! Owners Kenneth and Colleen Yoder will make breakfast for you and take you on a complimentary buggy ride. Kids are definitely welcome, and will enjoy the farm's steers, Percheron draft horses, chickens, fainting goats (yes, they *are* what the name implies), cats and dogs. This is the real thing. No electricity. No television. No phone. Just old-fashioned, traditional farm life.

1300 N 1000 W, Shipshewana
260.768.8086, ext 1

11

Wana frosty mug of root beer?

Generations have been raised on frosted glasses of homemade root beer, pizza burgers and Friday night fish at the Wana Cup. Located half-way between downtown and the Flea Market, it tempts many passers-by to grab a cool treat at the walk-up window. Their frozen treats include 50 flavors of home-made ice cream. The Wana Cup is a true Shipshewana blend of fast food paired with home-baked desserts.

295 S Van Buren St, Shipshewana
260.768.4923

12

Count the Yoders

Have you noticed a lot of businesses with similar names, especially "Yoder?" Inside Yoder's Shopping Center, the three businesses–Yoder Department Store, Yoder's Hardware and Yoder's IGA–are actually owned by different Yoders. And, Yoder's Meats and Cheeses down the road is owned by Bob Yoder, from yet a different family. Keep your eyes open, and you'll find many more Yoder businesses. In Shipshewana, the phrase "Keeping up with the Joneses" means much less than "Keeping up with the Yoders."

13

Add some *pop* to your corn in Indiana!

You can pick up Yoder Popcorn in many of the area stores, but it's extra special to visit the Yoder farm (yes, another Yoder!) several miles south of town. They always have fresh samples on hand, and offer all popping accoutrements: kernels, oils, seasonings, and poppers. Even microwave popcorn is available. Their specialty? A small kernel corn called Tiny Tender that's loved for being tender and having fewer hulls. The Yoders have been growing corn since 1936, and today they farm 1,000 acres.

7680 W 200 S, Topeka
800.892.2170
www.YoderPopcorn.com

14

The gallery that's as pretty as a picture

Galarina Folk Arts is a joy to visit. It is a fine arts gallery and shop located in the oldest building in town, the original train depot, circa 1888. The building is warm and welcoming, and the gallery is filled with artwork and unusual crafts from across the United States. Owned by Steve and Sheri Scott Welty, Galarina displays the largest selection west of the Hudson River of original paintings by Will Moses, great grandson of legendary Grandma Moses. Will is often on hand for book signings during MayFest and the Fall Crafters Fair. Sheri posts on the gallery's website the story of how her husband and she met Will: the story is a must-read before visiting the gallery.

Morton & Main, Shipshewana
260.768.4227
www.AmishArt.com

15

Store fronts and back roads

Only a small percentage of Shipshewana's one million visitors actually venture off the beaten path to find its lesser-known treasures. The back roads of Shipshewana are adorned with country stores, cottage industries and roadside stands filled with locally-grown produce and fresh-baked goods. Look for the signs, and stop in and take some time to visit. As it becomes harder to support families by traditional farming, the tourism trade actually helps local Amish families to maintain their chosen way of living.

16

Trails and trivia

Many locals don't know about the beautiful, wooded Culp Nature Preserve, even though it's only five minutes from downtown. Comprised of 20 acres, the preserve includes a half-mile walking trail. The preserve is known for its varied topography, wild ginger, wild leeks and great variety of wildflowers. Story has it that a natural spring flows half a mile south of the preserve, where in years past the Amish would stop to water their horses. To find the preserve, from SR 5, take US 20 west a mile and turn left/south on 900 W. The preserve is on the left about a mile down the scenic dirt road, in the midst of the wooded area. Some of the area's older residents know this as the "sink hole" road, but fear not; that problem was long ago fixed.

450 N 700 W, Shipshewana
260.637.2273
www.AcresLandTrust.org

17

Where the buffalo roam

Peter Cook followed a dream when he purchased his first herd of bison in 1998. The dream has grown from 30 to 300 head, and his family's farm has expanded from 83 to 900 acres, where all of the buffalo have plenty of room to roam. The farm is in Wolcottville, 25 minutes southeast of Shipshewana. Groups of ten or more can schedule tours for wagon rides into the pasture, followed by a "Cook-out" family picnic. The Cook's annual Calf Day Celebration in mid-June is a great opportunity to enjoy everything the ranch offers, including wagon tours, food, a petting zoo and live music.

5645 E 600 S, Wolcottville
260.854.3297
www.CooksBisonRanch.com

Chocolate cashew crunch.
Cinnamon caramel donuts.
'Nuff said.

Rise 'n Roll Bakery was once a small rural bakery on the Middlebury-Shipshe Road. Orvin & Viola Bontrager made scrumptious goodies that made those who knew about them oh, so happy. Then word got out, and they grew and grew and grew. So, Rise 'n Roll built a big, new building on US 20, just east of the LaGrange County line, where you can now enjoy breakfast and lunch in addition to picking up their time-tested sweet specialties. When you do something right, people notice. Hudsonville Ice Cream noticed, and they made an ice cream flavor using the bakery's highly addictive cashew crunch. Chicago has noticed, as Rise 'n Roll now has locations on Michigan Avenue and Clark Street. But you won't know all this from visiting the original local bakery; there, friendly faces let you know you're still in a small town.

1065 N 1150 W, Middlebury
574.825.4032
www.RisenRollBakery.com

19

Cupcakes in the Courtyard

Tucked in at the back of the Courtyard of Arts is the fun and festive Garden Gate Café, where owner Nancy Knobloch paints her part of the town pink. The café specializes in cupcakes and muffins, as well as fresh, savory food that ventures from the traditional starchy fare of the area. Nancy keeps things lively, with cook-outs and music on some summer evenings and frequent parties. When Nancy set up shop several years ago, her energetic spirit was felt throughout town. I love to share a meal with friends on the Garden Gate's shaded porch; it's a great place for people watching and relaxing.

125 Morton St, Shipshewana
260.768.7675
www.GardenGateCupcakes.com

20

Dig through 100 treasure-filled booths

I can spend hours in the Antique Gallery. Hours. The Gallery has grand, elaborate pieces of furniture and rare collectibles, as well as easily-affordable dishes, books and jewelry. The management is selective, so only quality antiques are sold by their more than 100 dealers who fill 31,000 square feet of gallery space. Everything is clean and organized, yet it still feels like you're digging through ages of treasures. The Gallery hosts two huge annual antique fairs and *An Evening at the Gallery*, where you can meet the vendors.

368 S Van Buren St, Shipshewana
260.768.7090
www.ShipshewanaAntiques.com

21

Taking care of one's own

Benefits and auctions are charitable and social events that bring the community together. The best of these worlds converge in several annual benefit auctions, where hundreds or thousands of people gather to eat great food and bid on items. The proceeds are used to take care of each other. Everyone is heartily welcomed, and you'll enjoy immersing yourself in local culture.

- Haiti Benefit Auction, June in Shipshewana
- Goldenrod Benefit Auction, August in Shipshewana
- Habitat for Humanity Auction, August in Shipshewana
- Michiana Mennonite Relief Sale, September in Goshen

22

Crrr-eak. Crreeeak.
(Find the best rocking chair in town)

Although Shipshewana is known for great shopping, not everyone can shop 'til they drop. Or, is it more that some just simply drop more quickly than others? All is well, as rocking chairs and benches are plentiful on porches and sidewalks throughout town. Some of the most "rocking" resting places are found at the Davis Mercantile and at the central hallway in Yoder's Shopping Center, where one can keep tabs on the comings and goings of locals and visitors.

Filigree lace eggs

Jerry Bontrager, born and raised in Shipshewana, uses tools akin to dentist drills to carve unbelievably intricate designs in real eggs, from tiny quail eggs to swan, goose, emu and large ostrich eggs. Jerry carves in his studio, Jerry's Eggs, which is at the Courtyard of Arts on Morton Street. He enjoys this hobby in his retirement, with varying hours, depending on the fishing forecast and his fancy (You may want to call ahead!). Jerry's always good for local lore and stories.

125 Morton St, Shipshewana
574.358.9241
www.JerrysEggs.com

24

Where the boys are…

Every good tourist town has at least one "guys' store," and in Shipshewana, Wellspring Components fits the bill. Alternative energy systems are important to Amish, vacationing RVers and those wanting to become more green. This store has solar panels, wind turbines, generators and every kind of battery you can imagine. Store owner Norman Yoder loves to talk about his power sources *and* about power grilling. He's collected a complete grilling line, with everything from ceramic, gas and charcoal grills to spices, sauces, accessories and cookbooks. He even rents grills of every size–basic units for small cookouts, chicken BBQ pits, or smokers and roasters for large events. Go ahead and try one. You'll be sure to impress everyone with your professional grilling equipment and expertise …at least for a weekend!

1085 N 850 W, Shipshewana
260.768.7336

25

Try your hand at cranking a corn sheller

Old Fashioned Farming Day is a dream come true for host Mervin Yoder. Merv has long been a collector of antique farm equipment. On the last Saturday of July, he and many other helping hands take visitors back in time half a century to watch as they do a full day of farming the old-fashioned way. Local resident SuEllen Yoder said her kids enjoyed riding the barrel train pulled by a refurbished John Deere tractor, and she and her husband, Leon, saw antique farming equipment that even they, as lifelong locals, couldn't identify. Plenty of homemade goodies are on hand to fill your belly, while steam engine-turned homemade ice cream and fresh baked pies top off your day. If you're not in town for this event, but would like to see Mervin's antique farm equipment, you're in luck, as he does offer tours by appointment.

260.768.4986
275 N 675 W, Shipshewana

26

Not just another sunset

While some places have a favorite vista, view or shore where you can savor the sunset, you'll find that the Shipshewana back roads provide countless pastoral scenes for sunrises and sunsets. The animals that work hard during the day seem especially restful at the quiet end of a productive day. Traffic moves slower, people talk longer and nature seems to sing a gentle lullaby, all against the pink and orange backdrop of a tranquil evening sky.

27

Let us introduce you to our friends

Bill and Sandi Miller have earned an excellent reputation by hosting visitors through their business, Buggy Line Tours. They offer short and long buggy rides, step-on guide services and back roads tours to watch noodle and cheese making, milking time on a farm, quilting, woodworking and buggy making. The Millers also transport guests to meals in Amish homes. Their tours are fun and relaxing, with many stories to hear and ample opportunities for visitors to ask questions. This is truly an extraordinary way to get a first-hand glimpse into local life. You can find Buggy Line's booth in the parking lot at Yoder's Shopping Center, or check out their comprehensive tour packages on their website.

888.442.8449
www.BuggyLine.com

28

Count the shades of "Amish Blue"

Sometimes people refer to a color as being "Amish Blue." I'm unsure which shade of blue *is* Amish Blue, and viewing the countless shades of blue fabric at Spector's doesn't help shed any light on the mystery, as they have more shades than Crayola could possibly collect. Spector's is a long-time staple for local shoppers, and, with three other stores located in Ohio Amish communities, is the closest thing I've found to being an Amish chain store. It's one of the places in town that Amish shop for their dry goods needs, including clothing, fabric and housewares.

305 S Van Buren St, Shipshewana
260.768.4439

29

Drive the Heritage Trail

This scenic winding loop is your voyage of discovery to area attractions, treasure-filled shops, historic stops, restaurants serving tasty Amish fare, lively downtown eateries and friendly faces at every turn. Following detailed directions on your vehicle's CD player, you'll experience seven unique communities—Shipshewana, Bristol, Elkhart, Goshen, Middlebury, Nappanee and Wakarusa—and reach every hidden corner of a region LIFE's editors selected among the 100 Places to See in Your Lifetime. Pick up a free audio tour CD and map at the Farmstead Inn or the LaGrange County Visitors Center, or download the audio instantly to your MP3 at www.AmishCountry.org.

Hats, bibs and bolts

Have fun taking your picture as you try on Yoder Department Store's more than 100 hats for sale, including Amish straw hats, top hats, prairie bonnets and felt fedoras. Buy a pair of Key bib overalls, from size 9 months to size 66. Indulge in over 12,000 bolts of fabric. Yoder's boasts over 60 years of selling goods to locals, and now to visitors, too. Basic? Unusual? You'll find it here!

300 S Van Buren St, Shipshewana
260.768.4887
www.YoderDepartmentStore.com

31

Challenge "Norm the Painter"

Norm says he'll paint on almost anything. Norm the Painter is actually Norm Klumpstra from LaPorte, Indiana, and he's been talking with visitors and painting at his booth at the Flea Market for more than a decade. His stock in trade is original paintings on windows, mirrors and saws using oil paint and O.F.S., which stands for "old family secret."

Shipshewana Flea Market
260.768.4129
www.ShipshewanaFleaMarket.com

32

Your thumb will be green with envy

You'll be wowed by the beautiful color combinations of the area's tidy flower beds and by the abundance of fresh produce grown in nearby gardens and fields. In the manner that quilters stitch together masterpieces of beauty from fabric, local gardeners create stunning outdoor artwork with blooms. Amish greenhouses yield healthy, gorgeous plants; visit one to pick up gardening tips and to purchase some living souvenirs from your visit. Check out one of the larger retailers, such as Cross Country Greenhouse, Lakeside Nursery and Nature Lane Greenhouse, or stop in at one of the small mom-and-pop nurseries you may discover scattered about around the countryside.

33

Meet Eva & Mariah

These gals are true celebrities in town. You'll see them outside the Blue Gate Restaurant at the carriage ride stand. Hundreds of people a day stop to whisper hello to them and to snap their photo. Though Shipshewana is undoubtedly more than a one-horse town, these lovelies are certainly the most photogenic.

Middlebury & Van Buren Streets, Shipshewana
888.447.4725
www.Riegsecker.com

34

Some might call it a furniture "factory"…

If you'd like to learn more about local furniture making, you can take a one-hour guided walking tour of Riegsecker Hardwoods. Daily tours start at 1pm. Watch as custom cabinets and handcrafted oak and cherry furniture are built step-by-step by local craftspeople. As Riegsecker Hardwoods is part of Riegsecker Marketplace, much of the furniture you'll see for sale at The Farm House, next to the Blue Gate Restaurant, is built in this shop.

5660 N SR 5, Shipshewana
888.447.4725
www.Riegsecker.com

35

Mush.
(Much tastier than its name implies!)

Mush is a thick porridge of cornmeal that's boiled in water, cut into slabs, and finally, like most prized local food, fried to a golden crisp. While mush is a staple found in every local eatery, the preferred style of serving it does vary. The basic version is to top it with butter and syrup, just as you would a pancake. Others swear of the supremacy of topping it with sausage gravy or tomato gravy. And yet others, though a decidedly smaller number, insist on topping it with headcheese. If you haven't heard of headcheese and what goes into making it, you may be better off not knowing, should you actually want to try it later. And, lastly, remember that we're in Indiana, where ketchup is an acceptable topper to every food item, including mush.

36

What will the bear wear?

Locals and visitors watch to see what the 8-foot carved bear in Orvan and Irma Lambright's yard will wear next. When an ice storm knocked down his tree several years ago, Orvan immediately knew that he wanted a bear to emerge from the stump. This is a very well-dressed bear. It has donned ears, tail and basket at Easter; a grass skirt and sunglasses in the summer; and has been both an angel and Santa for Christmas. Watch for the bear on the north side of US 20 between 925 W and 1000 W. In the fall you can see the bear up close if you stop in to buy cider from apples that Orvan grows and presses himself.

9655 W US 20, Shipshewana

The stories woven throughout the quilts

One of the area's exclusive treats is story-teller and collector Rebecca Haarer. She maintains a personal collection of historic vintage Amish quilts for educational purposes. A public collection of American vintage quilts, locally made traditional goods and old-world ornaments can be viewed and purchased at her downtown store on Morton Street. There, you will be greeted by Rebecca, her mother, Shirley, and the friendly creaks of the original hundred-year old wooden floors. To hear the stories first hand, groups of twelve or more can book an Amish Quilt Trunk Show.

165 Morton St, Shipshewana
260.768.4787

Quilt Gardens …along the Heritage Trail

17 supersized quilt-inspired gardens and 17 hand painted outdoor murals are "sewn" across the seven welcoming communities of Shipshewana, Bristol, Elkhart, Goshen, Middlebury, Nappanee, and Wakarusa. It's the only experience of its kind in the world and yours to enjoy at your own pace, absolutely free Memorial Day through October 1st. Detailed maps guide your way and are available at all garden locations, including Shipshewana's Menno-Hof and The Farmstead Inn. You can also download the details and read more about the project at www.AmishCountry.org.

Brisk action in the quiet days of winter

The streets and shops of town seem sleepy and still during wintertime, so it is a complete surprise to open the doors of the auction barn on Wednesday mornings and witness the antics and action happening inside. A cacophony of sounds and sights will greet you, as up to 10 auctioneers simultaneously rouse the crowds in their rings. The auction actually takes place all year long, as it has since the 1940's. This is a prime place for deal seeking and people watching. Antiques and miscellaneous items change hands to and from people from all over the country. Anyone can buy–just pick up a bidding number from the auction office. Beware of the contagious excitement, though. One winter day found me bidding aggressively and winning a trunk full of cement birdbaths and yard ornaments that neither I, nor my husband (who had to unload them) knew we needed!

345 S Van Buren St, Shipshewana
260.768.4129
www.TradingPlaceAmerica.com

40

Ride a rooster or a dappled gray mare

Get a bird's eye view of Shipshewana from the third floor of the Davis Mercantile while riding on the fully restored 1906 Dentzel Carousel. You can choose to ride atop a traditional carousel horse, or on a rural farm animal. This menagerie includes pigs, a rooster, sheep and several buggy horses. All animals were handmade and painted by local artists. The outer ring of animals were carved by a local Amish carver; be sure to take time to admire their handcrafted beauty.

225 Harrison St, Shipshewana
260.768.7300
www.DavisMercantile.com

41

Get the local "scoop"…

Stop at a shop where the locals go and pick up a local paper to get the inside scoop on auctions, sales, and events. *The Hometown Treasure* is a monthly paper for Shipshewana and Topeka residents; it includes "Hometown History" and other local columns. Several publications are specific to the Amish and Conservative Mennonite communities. *Die Blatt* features local news, and *The People's Exchange* serves northern Indiana and southern Michigan. *The Budget* is a national paper that has reports on local life from hundreds of Amish communities. The ads are great to read, too—I just read about an interesting new book called *The Chicken Came First;* I'm glad someone now knows.

…while you *have* a scoop of ice cream at the soda fountain

Emma isn't really a town—it's more of a four-way stop in the middle of the country—but it's pretty enough to tempt many wayfarers to visit time and again. On one of the four corners is the Emma Café, where you can get snacks and grocery items and sit down at the bar of the 1930's soda fountain for a sweet treat or a meal. Founded about 1860 just north of Emma Lake, the village was originally named Eden Mills because it had a large saw mill. By 1880, the town was renamed Emma after a beautiful woman who lived there. These days, Emma is such a popular girls' name that people often call the place "Emma Town."

5990 W 200 S, Topeka
260.593.9025
www.EmmaCafeAndCatering.com

43

Pedal the Pumpkinvine

Every third Saturday in June, around 1,000 people join in the annual Pumpkinvine Bike Ride. With various distances to choose from, this ride is suitable for families as well as the avid cyclist. It is a premier event that allows folks to view country farm life in action. The ride passes though small towns, past Amish country schools and meanders past scenic farms decorated with vibrantly colored flower gardens. Ample food is served along the way with a special dessert at the end. The ride's routes include portions of the new Pumpkinvine Nature Trail. While various parts are still under construction, once completed, this rails-to-trails project will stretch 17 miles through farm fields between Goshen, Middlebury and Shipshewana.

574.266.1362
www.Pumpkinvine.org

Down-home, In-home Amish dining:
The real deal.

Several Amish families in the area offer home-cooked meals for visitors. This experience is truly a treat and will be one of the most memorable moments of your visit. Reservations are required, and some places require a minimum number of guests, so the recommended way to book a meal is to do so through the LaGrange County Convention and Visitors Bureau. You're guaranteed not to leave hungry, and you'll likely feel as though you've made new friends from your time spent together.

45

B-eautiful B-Honey

Perry and Rosetta Bontrager have been keeping bees since 1986, and they now have a country store, B-Honey, to sell their own goods. They offer flavored honeys, lotions, lip balm and candles. They specialize in pure beeswax, which is even available in bulk. Want your own personalized candles? Bring in your own jars or containers, choose from 60 scents, and you'll be minding your own custom beeswax! The Bontragers also make and sell soy wax votives and jar candles, as well as apple cider vinegar, pressed from their own apples and aged in barrels.

2260 N 1000 W, Shipshewana
574.642.1145

History and mystery

The ornate splendor found in the St. James Chapel, settled on the well-groomed grounds of Howe Military School, is a style unlike anything you'll find in Amish Country. Built in 1902 as a model of a Cambridge chapel in Oxford, England, the chapel is listed on the National Register of Historic Places. Legend has it that the regal pews lining the walls were hand-carved by a German student in exchange for his tuition. The Chapel is steeped in rich history. Images of each bishop, and some of the school founders, including Mr. and Mrs. Howe, are enshrined with a stained-glass window. Stone stairs lead under the chapel to the crypt where lay the founders of the school. Free tours are available; please call ahead so they can have a tour guide waiting to tell you the intriguing stories of the chapel's enchanting history. Tours are also available in the Howe Mansion, which is also listed on the National Historical Register.

5755 N State Road 9, Howe
260.562.2131
www.HoweMilitary.com

47

Smell the smoke and hear the stories

While the common scene in Shipshewana is for men to be patiently waiting on women who are shopping, the men who find Jim Rubley at work may instead be the ones who need to be pulled away by waiting spouses. Jim is an historic blacksmith and can fill hours sharing his stories and knowledge. His small shed is filled with antiques and memorabilia. If he's in the shop, chances are you'll know by the smell of the smoke and the ring of the anvil.

In the alley east of Morton Street
Behind the Courtyard of Arts

48

Bigger than a barn door

Many people miss the impressive 12 x 24-foot mural in Yoder's Red Barn Shoppes. When you walk in, turn around and look up. You'll see a beautiful life-size harvest scene of an Amish farmer driving a team of three horses. The painting was created over the course of six months by local resident Rocky Weaver. The Red Barn is adjacent to the Flea Market, and is a nice, cool respite on a hot day, with three candy shops, locally made hardwood furniture, clothing, pretzels, toys, books and a friendly little deli.

445 S Van Buren St, Shipshewana
www.YodersRedBarn.com

49

Free road apples

Don't know what a "road apple" is? Travel the back roads behind a horse and buggy, and look down at the road: you'll soon figure it out. If you have a garden and are looking for some inexpensive fertilizer, go to Yoder's Shopping Center and fill up your pick-up truck with free horse manure. Manure from the hitching racks is collected and offered to the general public for free. While this practice may seem odd to some, gardeners know what a treasure this gift from Mother Nature is. We take "Reduce. Reuse. Recycle" to a whole new level.

Yoder's Shopping Center
300 S Van Buren St, Shipshewana

50

Connect the dots

Warren Street. Wayne Street. County Road 16. 250 North. Middlebury Street. There are many names for the road which connects downtown Middlebury and downtown Shipshewana, but most just call it the "Middlebury-Shipshe Road." I believe this is one of the prettiest lengths of straight road you'll find, and even though I travel it several times a week, I always enjoy the drive. You'll pass two Amish school houses, the cheese factory, roadside stands, beautiful Amish gardens, fields and farms. The new Pumpkinvine Nature Trail is approximately one-quarter of a mile north of the road, connecting Middlebury and Shipshewana for bikers and pedestrians.

Visit the vintage Hudsons

Enjoy a trip down memory lane as you examine over fifty fabulous antique Hudson vehicles exhibited at the Hostetler Hudson Auto Museum. Start with the beginning of the Hudson Company in 1909, wander through the Roaring '20s, and on to the Fabulous '50s. The museum is housed in the Shipshewana Town Center and is a hub for classic car lovers, who have the opportunity to explore five auto museums within a 40-minute drive.

760 S Van Buren St, Shipshewana
260.768.3021
www.HostetlersHudsons.com

52

Sweet treat tour

To get to the candy store at Plyley's, you walk through the middle of the candy factory, where you can see and smell all the sweet goodness created right in front of you. The Plyley family started making candy in 1917, and four generations later, Jack T. Plyley is still carrying on the family tradition. They specialize in chocolates and hard candy, and they hand make 1,600 to 2,000 pounds per day. Jack says the old-fashioned herb flavors—sweet clove, sassafras, horehound, and anise—are hard candy favorites.

909 S Poplar St, LaGrange
877.665.2778
www.PlyleysCandies.com

53

Whimsical woven wonders

In the same way that beautiful quilts emerge from the thrifty function of recycling fabric scraps, local weavers use left-over materials to create gorgeous woven rugs. Some sell the rugs in their shops that are scattered throughout the countryside, while others bring their wares to sell in town. Look for roadside signs of local weavers, such as Shady Ridge Weaving in Middlebury, Ruth's Weaving in Shipshewana, Yoder's Rug Weaving in Topeka and, by appointment, nationally-acclaimed Ragtime Rugs in Topeka. These rugs are long-lasting, soft, warm and functional pieces of art.

54

Sweet and salty

Vernon Miller has been popping up kettle corn for 13 years, and he says it's not just the yummy corn that keeps him making more, but the chance it gives him to talk to people from all over the world. Vernon always has free samples of cheddar cheese and traditional flavors on hand at his Blue Ribbon Kettle Korn stand. He sets up his copper kettle on the Flea Market side of the Red Barn on Tuesdays and Wednesdays, and at the front of the Red Barn other days. You'll enjoy the sweet and salty taste of Vernon's kettle corn as well as the flavor of the conversation.

Yoder's Red Barn Shoppes
www.YodersRedBarn.com

55

Blue skies. Blue fingers. Blue tongues…

If you drive north of town on SR 5, you'll see signs for several You-Pick blueberry patches. You don't need any experience to pick blueberries: just tie your bucket around your waist and head out into the blueberry bushes. Picking blueberries is less back-breaking than strawberry picking because the bushes are high enough that you don't have to bend over. This is a great outdoor activity for couples or for grandparents to take their grand kids. Kids love it because more berries pop into their mouths than into their pails! Not only are blueberries healthy, they freeze well and taste great over a bowl of homemade ice cream.

Oodles of noodles and buzzing beehives

Dutch Country Market is one of the largest country stores you'll find. It's owned by Norman and Katie Lehman, who work the store along with their children. You can often see Katie and the kids rolling out noodle-dough in their shop; talk about oodles of noodles, they make 400 pounds a day! Norman has tended bees for over twenty years and processes 36,000 pounds of honey products a year, including comb honey, honey sticks and nine flavors of whipped honey. The Lehman's market is filled with locally-made foods and crafts and even has a working beehive on display. During the summer, their outdoor stand holds locally grown produce and flowers. Dutch Country Market is on the Middlebury-Shipshe road, just two minutes east of Middlebury.

11401 CR 16, Middlebury
574.825.3594

57

How do we serve thee?
Let us count the ways.

The Blue Gate Restaurant is impressive in many ways, and here are a few fun facts and figures. Every year they serve 28.9 tons of mashed potatoes; 21.8 tons of roast beef; 31,332 whole chickens; 14.7 tons of lettuce; 15,871 dozen eggs; 7,200 slices of American cheese and 8,145 gallons of milk. From 2007 to 2009, they served 997,000 people. The restaurant seats 750 people. In the summertime, on a Tuesday or Wednesday (Flea Market days), they serve an average of 3,200 people per day. Equally impressive as these numbers are the restrooms. With vases of fresh cut flowers filling the countertops, it's no surprise that, in 2005, they were voted to have the 3rd best restrooms in America.

Middlebury & Van Buren Streets, Shipshewana
888.447.4725
www.Riegsecker.com

58

Play at the lake

Shipshewana Lake is a quiet lake. It's very uncommercialized and only a four-minute drive from downtown. You can rent canoes or kayaks by the hour from Arrowhead Recreation, or, if you're feeling ambitious, you can bicycle around the lake. There is a 4.5 mile loop from downtown – it doesn't always follow the lake, but it does take you through pretty countryside. Tuck a map in your pocket, and head west from the Blue Gate on the Middlebury-Shipshe road. Go north on 900 W and wind your way around the lake. Take a right on 350 N, go past the airport, right onto 850 W, back to the Middlebury-Shipshe road, and then left back into town. Reward yourself with pie.

9095 W 275 N, Shipshewana
260.768.4519
www.BrethrenRetreat.org

Follow the locals for flowers and produce

Sometimes locals take for granted the great opportunities we have at hand and only visit our local attractions when entertaining out-of-town guests. The long, expansive produce and plant aisle at the Flea Market is an exception, as many of us know it's an outstanding place to pick up bedding plants in the spring and produce throughout the summer. For those who may not have yet heard, Shipshewana has the Midwest's largest flea market, with 1,000 vendors spread over 40 acres. It's open only on Tuesdays and Wednesdays, May through October, and visited by 20,000 people each week.

345 S Van Buren St, Shipshewana
260.768.4129
www.ShipshewanaFleaMarket.com

60

Take a lick of the Cinnamon Stick

Just a picturesque ten-minute drive away, many people include Middlebury in their trip to Shipshewana. The Cinnamon Stick is one of the great finds in Middlebury. Built in 1890, it once housed a general store where eggs were "candled," and rope was measured by the foot and brought up through holes in the floor that are now plugged with Coca Cola bottle caps. The historic building now offers gifts from around the world, and packages are topped with real cinnamon sticks. The creative window displays are notable, and you can feel the charm and warmth the moment you step inside.

102 S Main St, Middlebury
574.825.7725
www.MyCinnamonStick.com

61

The better peanut butter

You'll probably first notice it on the tables in restaurants: a thick, creamy, smooth, sticky form of peanut butter. Once you try it, you'll start seeing it for sale everywhere, and you'll want to try all the different varieties of what is known as Amish Peanut Butter. Recipes vary but the main requirement is that it be unbelievably sweet. All recipes start with a base of store-bought peanut butter, and then the fun begins, by adding combinations of Karo syrup, maple syrup, corn syrup, marshmallow fluff or other sticky, sweet substances. Amish peanut butter makes everything it tops, even celery sticks, a treat!

62

You'll love what's in store for you

This small shop just north of the Middlebury-Shipshe road is a great example of a rural country store. Housed in an outbuilding on their farm, Freeman and Lizzie Yoder offer the utmost in personal service and quality products. Freeman, a polio survivor, opened the store in 1974 as a means for providing a livelihood for his family. The Yoder's store carries both basic staples and fun treats. You'll find locally made noodles, home remedies and herbs, housewares, Bibles and books, hand-drawn coloring books, children's toys and a great assortment of sundries. Local tidbit: as with many other area businesses, F & L's name is comprised of the couple's first initials.

55883 CR 43, Middlebury
574.825.7513 ext 1

Potato sack races

The annual MayFest celebration is a fun mixture of local festival and tourism season kick-off. While the shops have sales and specials, the town is filled with old-fashioned fun. The food tent is filled with locally-made concessions, and the entertainment tent is a popular destination with puppet shows and live music. The Saturday morning parade always boasts plenty of horses, wagons and tractors, and the old-fashioned kids games include sack races and wheelbarrow races. Everyone is welcome to join in on the fun and games.

800.254.8090
www.Shipshewana.com

Discover Das Dutchman

The beautiful grounds of Das Dutchman Essenhaus stretch over many acres, with walking paths, carriage rides, bicycle rentals, a covered bridge, miniature golf, gift shops, horseshoe pitching, a lovely inn and, of course, the famous Essenhaus restaurant. Owners Bob and Sue Miller treat guests to special events throughout the year: their events feature cooking, fashion, quilting and even classic car cruise-ins in the summer. The activities at the Essenhaus, 10 minutes west of Shipshewana, are varied enough to keep all aged members in your group entertained, and most offerings stay open throughout the evening hours.

240 US 20, Middlebury
800.455.9471
www.Essenhaus.com

65

Hum along or sing out loud

Those who have had the privilege of attending an Amish church service can attest to the power and simple beauty of Amish hymns. Congregants still use a 400 year-old hymnal, called the *Ausbund*, which is possibly the oldest Protestant hymnal in continuous use. The *Ausbund* uses no musical notation: the melodies have simply been remembered and passed down from generation to generation. Mennonite musical tradition also incorporates a cappella singing but has more variation than traditional Amish song. Learn about and listen to samples of these vocal traditions at Menno-Hof's exhibit called *A People Who Sing*, and pick up videos and music CDs in their gift shop. If, by chance or good fortune, you're offered an opportunity to hear local music live, by all means, do so.

510 S Van Buren St, Shipshewana
260.768.4117
www.MennoHof.org

66

How many sides?

If you ask locals the shape of the "Prough Barn," they'll either reply that it is octagonal, or they will answer "round." Historical records, however, state that it was built by Menno S. Yoder in 1908 as a model for a design of a *12-sided* concrete barn that he wanted to sell to farmers. Though Yoder's barn-making plans didn't take off, the barn is listed on the National Register of Historic Places and is the only polygonal barn in Indiana that is constructed of a material other than wood. 210 round and polygonal barns were built in Indiana from 1874-1936, perhaps more than any other state. While not open to the public, the barn is interesting to drive by and see; just go one mile west of the Blue Gate on Middlebury-Shipshe Road. Choose for yourself whether you'd call it octagonal or dodecagonal. "Round" might be the easiest answer.

250 N, one mile west of Van Buren St, Shipshewana

67

Homegrown and hormone-free

Yoder's Meat & Cheese Company raise their own beef cattle on their family farm and dry-age both corn-fed and grass-fed beef. All of their meats are naturally-fed with no added growth hormones or steroids. The Yoders operate their own smokehouse using real hickory and cherry wood chips, and they dry and smoke 17 varieties of jerky. The store carries over 100 varieties of cheese, as well as a wide array of jams, jellies, noodles, canned fruits and vegetables, seasoning sauces, bulk snack foods and candies. In other words, bring several coolers, because you'll want to take all this home with you. Their expansive store is located in front of the Flea Market, next to the Auction Restaurant. And if you're wondering about the Yoder name, this is the same family that has the Red Barn Shoppes, but not the Shopping Center.

435 S Van Buren St, Shipshewana
260.768.4715
www.YoderMeats.com

68

Bulk foods: quantity *and* quality

E & S Sales is a must-stop for many folks. You'll be amazed at the variety and quantity of bulk and discounted food. The staff measures and packages spices, flours, candies, soup and cooking bases, baking items and snacks. They stock over 50 different flavors of cheese at a discounted price, and several varieties are available to sample every day. Having opened in 1985 by Ervin Chupp, this impressive establishment has amassed a staff of over 55 people, and a wholesale list of more than 200 establishments.

1265 N SR 5, Shipshewana
260.768.4736

69

Lose yourself in aisles of fabric

The endless aisles of fabric found in town will inspire even non-sewers to dream up new projects just so they have an excuse to buy all the lovely designs. Calicoes and checks, florals and fleece, tidy bundled fatbacks and hefty brilliant bolts can also be found at small countryside fabric stores, like Laura's Fabrics outside of Middlebury or Creekside Fabrics in Emma.

- Lolly's Fabrics, Davis Mercantile
- Spector's Store, S Van Buren St
- Yoder Department Store, Yoder's Shopping Center

www.Shipshewana.com

Even the wind sings in Shipshewana

Making wind chimes is a labor of love for Orley Lambright. He found himself in the chime making business when his cousin needed a use for a load of square aluminum tubing. Orley now makes 29 different chimes from high-grade round and square tubing. The smallest chime, light and twinkly, is called *Ocean Breeze*, and the largest, at 84 inches, is the deep, mellow, *Music of the Universe*. Orley's personal favorite is *Hummer*, due to its long lasting resonance. Though Lambright Country Chimes has over 400 dealers nationwide, Orley and his family give one-on-one attention to each visitor who discovers his small showroom and workshop on his farm, just five minutes south of town.

0675 N 840 W, Shipshewana
260.768.7863 ext 2

Marvel at the making of the Mercantile

The historic Davis Mercantile and Davis Hotel, both Shipshewana fixtures since 1891, were destroyed by fire in 2004. The Davis Mercantile was re-built by local Amish men in the post & peg style, where native hardwood beams were cut and assembled much like Lincoln Logs. The pegs are the "nails" of this building. The Mercantile has an open staircase made of 4 native hardwoods. In the middle of the staircase is a 400 year-old Douglas Fir that can be seen towering through all four floors. You can count the rings yourself on a segment of the log that can be found at the base of the tree on the lower level of the building. Photos of this incredible building process are posted throughout this remarkable structure.

Harrison & Main Streets, Shipshewana
260.768.7300
www.DavisMercantile.com

Wildlife and natural splendor

The Pigeon River Fish & Wildlife Area is the largest nature preserve remaining in the Midwest, with over 11,500 acres, 17 miles of river, 266 acres of lakes and 356 acres of restored open water wetlands. Rent a canoe or kayak from the Senecal family at the Trading Post in Mongo, just 20 minutes east of town, and you'll be transported into a tranquil wonderland. Float up to 26 miles on the lazy, meandering river and see very few signs of civilization, but don't be surprised if you're greeted by beavers, otters, osprey, pike, trout and eagles. The Trading Post has been

family-owned since 1971, and their campground and rental services are available seven days a week, April through October.

7525 E 300 N, Mongo
260.367.2493
www.TradingPostCanoe.com

73

Creative concoctions for kids of all ages

The makeup stations at Judy Yoder's Lotions and Potions store are kid-sized and full of sparkly options. Grab an ice cream scoop full of pastel-colored sugar scrub and top it with sprinkles to make a personalized skin care sundae; pump out your favorite shade of lotion and add in enough glitter to make a fairy princess shimmer; and mix up the prettiest tints of lip balm, eye shadow or blush, and you'll have as much pint-sized glamour as a girl can handle. Judy also has scrumptious options for grown-ups, with almost 500 scents that she can add to hair, face and skin care products. She may even let the "big kids" add some glitter to their products, if they ask nicely.

Yoder's Red Barn Shoppes
800.981.9478
www.LotionAndPotion.com

Create a custom cutie

The gals at Kids Kreations will help you create an 18, 20 or 22-inch doll for someone you love, young or old, or even for yourself. You select the face, skin tone, eyes, hair and clothes, and in 30 minutes, the doll is all yours, complete with a birth certificate. Sisters Mary and Edna make this fun experience unforgettable; it seems there is always a lot of laughter in this store. You can make a reservation, or just stop in. You can also book a doll-making party at the shop, or they can bring the fun to you at a hotel or home.

150 N Harrison St, Shipshewana
260.768.7744
www.BabyBuzz.net

Get caught with your hand in the candy jar

The third floor of the Davis Mercantile is a prime destination for kids, with Aunt Millie's Candy & Nut Shop, the toy store, and the carousel all being within earshot of parents. Aunt Millie's has an old-fashioned candy counter with ample amounts of candy, both nostalgic and novelty, for keeping the day extra happy. Make sure you buy a bag for the ride home, too.

Davis Mercantile, 3rd floor
260.768.7728
www.AuntMilliesCandy.com

Marlene's brush with frame

Marlene's paintings are sold far and wide. Her favorite subjects are scenes from nature or of her Amish heritage, and she paints on site from her studio located in the Courtyard of Arts. Raised in Shipshewana, Marlene's brother Chris owns Creekside Bookstore on SR 5 north of town; her brother Noah owns Nature Lane Greenhouse in the countryside northeast of town; and her brother Marty owns The Wana Cup. All of the siblings are gracious hosts and provide warm conversation.

Tiffany's in Topeka

The food is always good at Tiffany's, and the pie is always superb. Locals as well as visitors who are "in the know" don't hesitate to make the ten mile drive south of Shipshewana to eat there. The food isn't fancy; it's local fare, cooked up right. Home cooked food, casual atmosphere and endless hospitality add up to a terrifically tasteful time at Tiffany's. To find Tiffany's Restaurant, go south out of town on SR 5 for seven miles, then east two miles on 700 S. It's worth the trip. Be sure to leave room for pie.

414 E Lake St, Topeka
260.593.2988

If barns could talk

The barn on the Amish farmstead at B & L Woodcrafts, built in 1940, presents a rare opportunity for those who want to see the inside of an actual barn. Owners Betty and Lyle have filled the barn with antiques, gift wares, wooden drying racks and lawn accessories; the deeper you delve, the more you see. The beams and rafters speak to years of providing shelter, while marks on the floor just inside the door tell the tale of the added "umph!" demanded of the horses as they pulled heavy hay wagons up the ramp and into the barn. B & L is on the Middlebury-Shipshe road, about four minutes west of town.

10045 W 250 N, Shipshewana
888.642.6016

Family-style dining…
and *they* do the dishes!

When you see a restaurant offering "family-style" dining and you have several people in your party, you should take the plunge and try it. The Blue Gate's description: "Experience a traditional Amish meal just like we serve in our homes, with the selection of a buffet, brought tableside in bowls and platters." Tender roast beef, homemade meatloaf or smoked ham, fried chicken, real mashed potatoes, chicken dressing, gravy, vegetables, homemade noodles, a fresh garden salad, homemade bread, and your choice of pie, bread pudding or ice cream, completed with the four magical words, "all you can eat."

www.BlueGateRestaurant.com

From herd to curd

Formerly named simply Deutsche Kase Haus, which is Pennsylvania Dutch for "The Cheese Haus," this business's new name includes "Guggisberg," the name of their new owners. Cheese making hours are 8am-noon on weekdays, but call ahead to make sure, so you can see the cheese being made, step by step, using local milk. Many cheeses are on hand to sample, including their world champion Colby. Some other notable favorites are yogurt, salsa, Swiss, Pepper Jack, butter, rye and vegetable cheeses. Their great gift shop sells more than cheese. They also carry souvenirs, noodles, meats, jams and jellies, candy and toys. They're located four miles west of town on the Middlebury-Shipshe road.

11275 W 250 N, Middlebury
574.825.9511
www.BabySwiss.com

Find the prettiest shed, miles from nowhere

The Garden Shed is the best little surprise. If you go south one mile from Emma on 600 W, after winding around Emma Lake, you'll see a small sign directing you to take the curve left onto 300 S. Follow it, and you'll find an actual garden shed, surrounded by beautiful gardens and filled with baskets, soaps, linens and dried flowers. Located on the farm of Chris Jr. & Edith Lambright, the shed is open when they're at home. This place truly is a delightful discovery out on the back roads.

5775 W 300 S, Topeka

82

Cool treats in the country

Lucy's Twist is a small family-owned ice cream stand that usually has a good-sized crowd when it's hot outside. While it seems as though this obscure place is in the middle of nowhere, it's actually just a mile south of US 20 in LaGrange, on the road named 00EW because it is the center point in the county from which all north/south roads get their names. The prices are low, whole-family friendly, the servings generous and the surroundings will melt your heart but, hopefully, not your ice cream.

955 S 00 EW, LaGrange
260.463.3868

83

Blooming where they are planted

Take notice of how clean and pristine the farms are in northern Indiana. Everything is in order and in its place. Even the gardens grow tight and tidy, as straight rows of clean, colorful flower beds frame the bountiful vegetable plants. Cleanliness is next to Godliness here, pure and simple.

Bountiful Bonneyville Mill Park

If it's a pretty day, any time of the year, head to Bonneyville Mill Park, 12 minutes west of Shipshewana. This park has it all: 223 acres, a climbing tower, sledding hills, meadows, river banks, cross country skiing trails, woods, picnic shelters, marshes, seven miles of hiking trails, dahlia and herb gardens, a one-room school, festivals, wildlife, wildflowers and a 150 year-old water powered mill.

53373 CR 131, Bristol
574.535.6458
www.ElkhartCountyParks.org

Christmas shopping to savor

Christmas time in Shipshewana is quiet, relaxed and yet, festive. The shops get into the spirit with decorations and lights, and occasionally, carolers or street musicians add the sweet sound of holiday song. Bundle up for a buggy or sleigh ride. A "Light Parade" in November ushers in the holiday season, and an Ice Festival between Christmas and New Year's brings perfect timing for outdoor fun during Christmas vacation.

86

Spicy Shipshewana?

In general, local fare is not known for its spicy flair, but it's a different story for Kevin Horn and his Shipshewana Spice Company. Kevin has been offering over 200 spices, seasonings, herbs and extracts for 30 years at the Flea Market. Kevin is most famous for his *Happy Salt* blend, but I know of a woman from Alaska who always makes a point to pick up another kind, the *Midwest Blend*. I guess the variety really is the spice of life.

345 S Van Buren St, Shipshewana
260.768.4129
www.ShipshewanaFleaMarket.com

87

Everything you do
(or don't necessarily) need

When asked to describe what people will find at Yoder's Hardware, owner Winford Jones said, "People sometimes call us a treasure chest. Well, we're more than a hardware, and we're more than housewares. We have things you need, and we have things you don't need. But it's still fun to look around." Find cast-iron cookware, garden seeds sold by the scoop and farming and livestock gadgets so unusual that you may only be able to guess at their function.

300 S Van Buren St, Shipshewana
877.988.9309
www.YodersHardware.com

88

Picnic with lions, & tigers, & bears, *oh my.*

Just ten minutes south of Shipshewana, you'll find Maple Lane Wildlife Park, located on an Amish farmstead. Owners Lavern and Ruth Anna Yoder offer a petting zoo, pony cart and camel rides, and a picnic area. Take a self-guided tour through the shaded wildlife grounds to view the animals up close. You'll see an assortment of exotic animals such as rheas, cougars and monkeys, along with local farm animals and wildlife. Maple Lane is open Tuesday through Saturday, Memorial Day weekend through Labor Day.

7410 W 700 S, Topeka
260.593.2248

A slice of the good life

As American as apple pie is, strawberry and blueberry pies are actually the top sellers at the Shipshewana Auction restaurant, where they sell over 25,000 slices each year. Tressie, a local Amish woman, has made the majority of pies herself over the past 28 years.

Here are some of the local places known for their pie:

- Shipshewana Auction Restaurant
- 5 & 20 Country Kitchen
- Blue Gate Restaurant
- Bread Box Bakery
- Country Corral
- Daily Bread
- Wana Cup
- *and in the summer,* the Red Bud Café

90

Dirt. Smoke. Boys and Grandpas.

Abandoned machines that were once a farmer's pride and joy are dressed up, painted, and made to sing by someone who sees the beauty in a forgotten hunk of metal. These are the stars of the Northeast Indiana Steam and Gas Engine Show held every year in August at the LaGrange County 4-H Fairgrounds. Spending the day with the smoke, the dirt, the stories and the irreplaceable camaraderie is a way for grandpas to forge a link with the next generation, who otherwise might not know what it was like "way back when."

1030 E 75 N, LaGrange
888.277.3184
www.VisitShipshewana.org

91

Shop in your pajamas

Silks and satins, flannels or fleece, shopping in your pajamas is really only socially acceptable to do one day a year, Pajama Sale Day, which is usually the first Saturday in February. Specials and sales start in the wee hours of the morning, and the hotels are packed with people having overnight parties beforehand. We've even seen limousines unload a pack of pajama-clad bargain hunters. This is the only time of the year when the shoppers are up and at it earlier than the farmers.

92

Cabbies always have the best tales

The buggy drivers have the greatest stories and know the local lore. Buggy, carriage and sleigh rides are available around town and throughout the countryside. Take a long ride, and ask the driver what you'd really like to know!

- Buggy Lane Tours, 877.825.5474
- Buggy Line Tours, 888.442.8449
- Countryside Buggy & Sleigh Rides, 877.593.2640
- Riegsecker Carriage & Pony Rides, 888.447.4725

93

What'll ya give me for this beauty?

See a horse, buy a cow, sell a sheep (or just come to watch the action). Maybe you don't have room in the car to take home something from this auction, but watching the auction rings is something people of all ages enjoy. Farmers from Michigan, Ohio and all over Indiana come here each week to buy and sell. Wednesdays livestock auctions are for pigs, sheep, lambs, goats, cows and hay; Friday auctions are for horses ...driving, draft, saddle and ponies. I always bring my visiting friends and family to the auction, at least for a few minutes, to get an inside glimpse of this timeless rite of farm life.

345 S Van Buren St, Shipshewana
260.768.4129
www.ShipshewanaFleaMarket.com

Horse Stories

Peter and Elaine Stone are blessed to be able to build their lives around their passion – the world of horses. Peter's father, Sam, started the first model horse company in 1950, and Peter carries on the tradition with Stone Horses. Their factory and showroom are located on the north side of town. Take a free tour of the factory to see artists painstakingly hand finish and paint details on the model horses. Tour times are 1pm Monday-Friday. Stone Horses are known world-wide for their detail and artistry. Many horse lovers visit the Stone Horses showroom or website to design a horse that looks like their own. Young enthusiasts can try their hand at painting their own model at one of the two annual shows in town.

805 E North Village Dr, Shipshewana
866.581.1370
www.StoneHorses.com

The stories of the town and its people

In a town with a population of around 500, people know each other, as well as their stories. One of the town's best keepers of the stories, known for her spunk and for her big heart, is Gladys Ringo. Gladys has been Shipshewana's special correspondent to *The Goshen News* and *The LaGrange Standard* for as long as I can remember; she's a contributing author to *The Story of Shore Mennonite Church* and *Shipshewana 1889-1989, a Patchwork Sampler*; and she has published a sizeable assemblage of photos, stories and articles she has collected over the years, entitled *Memorable Events & Citizens of Shipshewana*, which can be found in local stores. If you want to learn more about Shipshewana's stories, past or present, pick up a copy of Gladys' book. Every town needs a keeper of the stories. We've got Gladys!

96

The fabric of our society

Several days after the Davis Mercantile burned to the ground, a local resident found a scrap of charred calico fabric clinging to a nearby bush. It was identified as coming from Lolly's Fabrics, which perished in the fire. The project designer of a quilt commissioned for the new town offices invited quilters to incorporate the piece into the Blessing Quilt, which you can view at the Town Hall. It draws its design from Potawatomi bead work and Amish quilt patterns, honoring two groups which have significant local cultural heritage. If you look closely, you may find the postage stamp-sized scrap of calico that survived the fire. Each year the Farmstead Inn selects a block from the quilt for their Quilt Garden design.

345 Morton Street
www.Shipshewana.org

97

A hearty harvest

I have to admit that I have to repeatedly ask the difference between hay and straw. And, even having lived in the area most of my life, I truly couldn't tell you what crop is growing in a given field or the names of the implements the farmers are using to harvest them. I can tell you, though, that seeing generations of farmers work together to gather and process crops always makes me smile. Slowing down for wagons and tractors on the road is a blessing sometimes when we need reminders to take a break from the hectic pace of our lives. Just as springtime brings smiles with scenes of newborn colts and calves and the sowing of seeds, autumn in rural farming country brings a satisfied glow in viewing scenes of neat rows of haystacks and a job well done.

Kids + men + toys = more time to shop

Dad's Toys is a favorite place for the guys to hang out, with scale model cars, toys, model horse drawn vehicles, model horses, John Deere and sports merchandise, and lodge and wilderness decor. Add to it a full size antique tractor and car and a live miniature horse to pet and feed, and you've just bought yourself a few more shopping hours 'cause the guys and the kids will be entertained for quite awhile here.

215 N Van Buren St, Shipshewana
888.447.4725
www.Riegseckers.com

Staged for delight

The Blue Gate Theater showcases quite a variety of programs throughout the year: Southern gospel, family-friendly comedy shows, bluegrass, country and even storytelling sessions grace their stage. Holiday-themed shows are always offered, with dinner/show combos available for the "big" holidays of Valentine's Day, Christmas and New Year's Eve. The theater is elegant, and there isn't a bad seat in the house. If you're looking for something to do in the evening, you should definitely check out what's showing. The performances are always family-friendly, and matinee shows during peak visitor season mean everybody gets a chance to enjoy the show.

Middlebury & Van Buren Streets, Shipshewana
888.447.4725
www.Riegsecker.com

A patchwork of quilting events

Shipshewana's rich quilting heritage and access to some of the country's best quilt and fabric shops brings groups and individuals to our quilt festivals, auctions and retreats.

- Honeyville Quilt Auctions, Annually, April & September
- Shipshewana Quilt Festival, Annually, June
- Topeka Quilt Show & Sale, Annually, June
- Quilting Bees at the Carriage House
- Amish Quilt Trunk Shows by Rebecca Haarer

New events and opportunities arise frequently. Call the LaGrange County Convention and Visitors Center for more details on planned events or to schedule your own retreat.

800.254.8090
www.VisitShipshewana.org

101

Slow down, take it easy

Things move slower in Shipshewana, and that's one of the main reasons people come here. The roads here are filled with bikes, buggies, people walking and kids on pony carts, so please take extra caution as you travel. Be sure to slow down as you're driving, for the safety of others and for more chances to take in the beauty all around you. And slow down when you're walking; take time to look around. Smile at others, and you'll be sure to receive smiles in return.

Index

Photo credits